I'm No Lady
When Objects Have Women's Names

© 2002 Triennale di Milano
All rights reserved

Printed in Italy
ISBN 88-8158-385-2

Edizioni della Triennale

Fondazione La Triennale di Milano
viale Alemagna 6
20121 Milano
tel. +39-0272434.1
fax +39-0289010693
www.triennale.it

Edizioni Charta
Via della Moscova 27
20121 Milano
tel +39-026598098/026598200
fax +39-026598577
email: edcharta@tin.it
www.chartaartbooks.it

Permanent Collection of Italian Design

Non sono una signora
Quando gli oggetti hanno un nome di donna

Palazzo della Triennale
23 January – 21 April 2002

Curator
Silvana Annicchiarico

Exhibition Installation
Giancarlo Basili

Graphic Project
Daniele Mastrapasqua

Setting-up of Exhibition
Produzioni Reali

Cover
Carlo Mollino, *Gilda*, 1954
Zanotta Collection

Back cover
Rita Hayworth in *Gilda*, 1946

LA TRIENNALE DI MILANO

PERMANENT COLLECTION OF ITALIAN DESIGN

JK

COLLEGE OF ART AND DESIGN

I'm No Lady
When Objects Have Women's Names

edited by Silvana Annicchiarico

CHARTA

Indice

Public and Private

Augusto Morello
President of the Milan Triennale

The fact that an everyday object is invented with performance in mind and innovated for the sake of semiology is not a recent discovery but only (relatively) recently acknowledged, duly studied and explicitly put into practice.

The function of form is now juxtaposed with the form of function; even though it does not often shrewdly imitate the title of a famous old book: *Il significato del significato* (The meaning of meaning).

And not infrequently attending to syntactic relations in the context of imagined reality; that reality which—when absent—translates a group of objects which may be individually "beautiful" into a whole which might be ugly, as we unfortunately see happening every day.

However, of all the eras, ours is the one in which everyday objects are most public—be it because of their diffusion, be it because of their (at least) ostentatious use—whose meanings are as "external to need" as they are understood to be "internal to desire." This is true for the user/owner/exhibitor who—above all in his role of owner/proprietor and future (or so it seems) mere renter—experiences, in and with the commodity he has made his own, a secret domesticity, a confidential fondness, a privacy; sentiments, memories, intimacies—that only he can (and sometimes does not wish to) describe—cling to the object.

But the designer too—before the manufacturer—attributes private values to the fruit of his efforts due to a space, a time, a particular circumstance of "his" every-day life. And one of these "private impulses," whether it be the designer's purpose or due to his delicacy, is the attribution of a name, often the name of a woman, which means a great deal to him; while for others it may be little more than an indicator of diversity.

The names of objects therefore end up inhabiting that semiological limbo which lies between the private and the public and, when all is said and done, between the meaning and the sense. Some suppose it to be a discrepancy; giving a product a name becomes a fashion, an affectation, even a mere aid to competitiveness, of *captatio benevolentiae*.

This (first) exhibition for a museum of design—an exhibition of names rather than things—intends to spark off a new inquiry into the meaning and sense of objects, or rather into the profundity of everyday life.

And, just as Kafka said to Milena that only she could distinguish "the in-spite-of-all from the great nevertheless," it is no coincidence that this idea should have been chiefly female.

Names and Things

Ugo Volli
University of Turin

Und dennoch sagt der viel, der "Abend" sagt
Ein Wort, daraus Tiefsinn und Trauert rinnt
Wie schwerer Honig aus den holen Waben
H. Von Hohmansthal - *Ballade der äusseren Leben*

And anyway whoever says "evening" says much
A word from which depth and sadness flow
Like heavy honey from hollowed-out honeycombs

What relationship is there between names and things? Is there a "true name" which "rightly" says the thing it names? Are names images or labels? Do they classify the world or our mental states? Do they add something to reality or merely mirror it? In European culture the philosophy of language is born of these problems and continually returns to them.

To give just a few prescribed examples, at the beginning of the bible (Gen. 2:19) immediately after the event of creation we read: "Now the Lord God had formed out of the ground all the beasts of the field and all the birds of the air. He brought them to the man to see what he would name them; and whatever the man called each living creature, that was its name." It seems a simple solution, like the mythical language it is wrapped up in, and yet the myth in its turn is very problematic. There should be names which belong to things in a strong sense, which represent them unequivocally. But these have been assigned by man or rather the first man to encapsulate the whole of humanity. We are the ones who give the "right" names to things. But how? For a long time religious thought questioned itself about the "right" language spoken by Adam; Dante also returned to the question twice (in *De vulgari eloquentia* and in *Commedia)* suggesting different solutions, first Hebrew then a special language, lost forever.

And there is also the problem of knowing if our common progenitor had *identified* names inherent in things, using the superior intelligence of the state of Eden, or whether he had simply made a decision, using his authority as world patriarch. Is naming an act of dominion a sort of scientific discovery? The most plausible example of "true names" we can refer to today, after all, is that of scientific terminology: H_2O is a better name than water, because it tells us something about the substance, it corresponds therefore to an affirmation, it names a liquid composed of a molecule of oxygen tied to two molecules of hydrogen. And from this point of view a kind of name diagram, part icon, appears to work even better.

So the notion of a true or right name does not seem so crazy, apart from containing some "truth" about its object. But this too is a dangerous argument because we normally tend to think that the truth regards mainly affirmations (or, technically, utterances, and not names).

$$H \searrow O$$
$$H \nearrow$$

Plato's *Cratilus* unfolds not far from these themes. This is the work that inau-

gurates the Western philosophy of language. The dialogue opens with a pro-
grammatic declaration (383a): "Cratilus maintains that there is a correct name
naturally inherent to every thing. In his opinion the true name is not the one
you give a thing by speaking, on the basis of an agreement; he means precisely
to say that things have a natural name, the same for the Greeks and for the
Barbarians."

It is evident, however, that in reality names of things are not the same for the
Greeks and Barbarians, indeed in reality different languages usually call things
in different ways and the Italian word "cane" is "dog" in English, "hund" in
German, "perro" in Spanish, "kelev" in Hebrew, "sobaka" in Russian.... This obvious practical difficulty and other problems of a theoretical nature induce Plato
himself, at the end of *Cratilus*, to refuse a naturalistic theory of the name, to
which he yet felt inclined. Plato is forced to admit that there is a historical
dynamic of language and he makes an effort to climb the etymological chain
until he reaches the original gesture of a *nomothétes*, a legislator of language
who, like Adam in the dominion hypothesis, authoritatively decided the names
of things, doing so however on the basis of a certain knowledge, a competence
regarding the truth analogous to that of the chemist and water. In the form of
names, in the almost physical sense that the different sounds carry, we might
perhaps discover once again the ancient truth of the *nomothétes*.

With a sarcastic taste for the intellectual paradox, Plato prolongs the game until
hinting at a sort of small treatise of fantastic etymology, though showing us
that, in reality, the game doesn't work: language is too malleable and contra-

dictory to appropriate a rigid classification of the world, in research one soon has to make contradictory assumptions. Reduced to the qualities one can draw from their form, names reveal a labyrinthine if not contradictory organization of the world. And if a name were really perfect, if, that is, it were able to repeat all the properties of its object, Plato objects, wouldn't this perhaps be a second thing, a replica or a twin, in any case, a very different thing from a name? Isn't a partial inadequacy, a certain imperfection, therefore, part of the very nature of the name?

Aristotle (*Perì ermeneias* 16a) believes he can establish that, in general, "the sounds of the voice are symbols of the affections of the soul and written letters are symbols of the sounds of the voice. But letters are not the same for everyone and neither are sounds; and anyway sounds and letters are signs of the affections of the soul, which are identical for everyone and constitute the images of objects which are already identical for everyone." This is the first explicit affirmation on that property of historical-natural languages which today we tend to call, using Ferdinand de Saussure's terminology, "arbitrariness," and which appears to be the general foundation of the most important properties of language, of its complex play with reality.

We must make a distinction however: taken in its Aristotelian version, the arbitrariness of language detaches itself from a world of *given* things which are the "same for everyone," represented simply through different "sounds of the voice," due to the plurality of men—as sounds are not the "same for everyone." The fact is that both things in the world and the names which are assigned to them have an objective statute in common, they are already there, the first universal while the second different in different languages, but both *given*. Aristotle believes there is only one grid, common to all men, which analyzes reality; that sounds, corresponding to things, should vary is an accident which, all things considered, means little, seeing that not only things but also the mind's ideas are the same.

Twentieth-century linguistics, at least in its structuralist version, adopted a much more radical position: it is not just written letters and vocal sounds but also mental images and even world objects that are variable. That something is a dog, as opposed to a fox, a wolf, a coyote and other similar animals, is a biological fact; but different societies might place greater or lesser value on this fact and therefore either construct, or not, peculiar "mind affections" for this or that category of objects and then find a name for such an "affection" (or perhaps it is the opposite: find a name first and then allow it to shape an idea). Other categories of objects are, on the other hand, completely artificial: there is no natural basis for the distinction between chairs and armchairs, or between assemblies and councils, between loving and falling in love. It is all the more natural to think in these cases that language creates the idea, and that the historical modification of values and linguistic habits modifies the meaning of ideas and the very definition of "things" which should be "represented" by the word. Language is not essentially a nomenclature. Meanings are formed in a more complex, syntactic, structural fashion because of the implicit comparison with terms that do not appear in any concrete expression. The hypothesis of a creator of language, which assigns names to things, present in both biblical and platonic myth, serves to bridge the enigma of the origin of language. We know that things can be called in different ways, but how did it happen that out of all the different possibilities these prevailed? What is the reason behind a gesture—the naming—that we must always suppose to be antecedent to language, even though this appears to be the linguistic action par excellence, the one which inaugurates language? (This contradiction in the idea of an original naming, both on a phylogenetic and ontogenetic level is the gist of Wittgenstein's objection towards the Augustinian theory of language acquisition, at the beginning of *Philosophical Works*: how can we learn to speak by simply indicating things and emitting the corresponding sound, if we are lacking the linguistic frame from which the sound might draw meaning?)

Understanding how humanity's original lexicon is shaped (if one or many, if limited to a series of names of things or instead dominated by the emotion of the speech act) is a task equivalent to the quest for the origin of language—a theme which scientific linguistics has forbidden since it was formed. But there are specific, partial lexicons which are continually formed before our very eyes and evolve ceaselessly. For example, the scientific and technological field produces a terminology which is constantly evolving; but this also happens, according to considerably different principles and modalities, in other areas of "modern" life, from sport to the economy to commodity economics in general. If we consider these to be mechanisms of linguistic formation, it is easier to see a broad heterogeneity. There are expressions which are born "cultured," due to the composition of meanings drawn from the classical languages, which however become naturalized and lose the link with their past. Think of the series of compounds with the Greek "tele" (telephone, television, etc., which then give rise to abbreviations like TV or derivatives) or the strange story of the fax, which actually derives from a Latin imperative ("fac-simile") contracted and processed into the object. There are increasingly frequent cases of contemporary language loans, usually from more prestigious and widespread languages: for Italians two centuries ago it was French while today it is English. We can add compound nouns (the word for "tomatoes" in Italian is "pomodori" which literally means "golden apples"), metaphors (the "charm" of elementary particles), figurations, exchanges, initials, every form of manipulation of the signifier.

In the case of commercial products, the process of inventing names has been a commercial technique for some time, bound to marketing considerations and obeying the rules which protect the competition, brand ownership and copyright. It thus happens that certain graphic-verbal combinations which sound efficient (for example, those containing many letter Xs) are destined for the pharmaceutical industry, above all if they do not present upsetting semantic associations in any of the major international languages; while car manufacturers combine words which already exist in various languages, deforming them in the belief that they will avoid ambiguities and negative impressions, and patenting them to name their vehicles. In all this there is something of platonic *nomothétes*—but it is a seductive *nomothétes*, which thinks, in the modern manner, of the budget and the emotive impression it has to correspond to rather than the substance of the object and the truth of the name.

However bizarre or inventive these linguistic creations might be, they are however becoming part of every language and, in order to be successful, have to follow the rules of the language. They are, that is, forced to assimilate themselves to their more traditional elements. Generally this means nouns, because it is more common to have to deal with new objects and, perhaps, commercial products which are to be launched on the market, rather the qualities (adjectives) or actions (verbs) which usually follow on from objects or are re-elaborated by already existing linguistic units, even though their linguistic function is not at all secondary. Thus we speak of "airplanes" but "flying," "Internet" but "surfing," and different models of cars all demand to be "driven." New objects are therefore all connected to nouns. It is not so important to establish whether we are dealing with "proper" or "common" names, a distinction which grammar makes in principle, without really succeeding in separating the two categories. It often happens that a commodity's proper name (that is a company trademark) becomes able, thanks to its success, to name the whole commodity genre (just think of "jeep," "Magnetophon," "PC," "walkman"). And a re-appropriated common noun is often used as a proper name—from *Bianca* (white) and *Regina* (queen), used as female proper names for detergents like *Dash* and *Tide*). In any case, once they have entered into the lexicon, the names must follow the rules of the language. To work as a subject they must, for example, define themselves in terms of number, that is acknowledge a singular or plural; they must be animate or inanimate, more or less capable of certain actions, that is more or less susceptible to relationships with certain verbs. The car, in our culture, whether it be a Ferrari or a *Seicento* (a Fiat model), is almost animate, it has a sort of mechanical life, and therefore it can "run" or "stop," "be impatient" or "strong," which is unlikely to happen in the case of a television or armchair.

In particular, in the majority of European languages (but not in English for example), names have a gender. Common nouns have a gender, so that in Italian, for no plausible reason, tables are masculine and chairs feminine, while in German, so much for the raptures of poets and astrologers, it turns out that the sun is feminine (*die Sonne*) and the moon is masculine (*der Mund*). In Italian books are masculine while encyclopedias are feminine; plates are masculine while pans are feminine, walls are masculine while windows are feminine, the fax, the computer and the mobile phone are all masculine while the photocopier, the dishwasher and the car are all feminine. The sword, the spear, the club and armor are feminine; the shield and the gun are masculine....

All this might seem embarrassing in an era of political correctness, when the equanimity towards gender is not only an ethical and political imperative of respect for people's rights, but also, in certain countries, an obligatory grammatical requisite of the language—certainly more difficult to apply in Italian, in French or in German than in English. But it is also an opportunity. Because in these languages naturally endowed with gender there are also proper names which certainly help to create a play of homogeneity or detachment, between trademarks and types of commodity, linguistic inventions and a shared frame of reference.

And because the grammatical reference to a gender is certainly something very different from the attribution of an actual sex to objects. And anyway gender is never a purely abstract mark; it facilitates the attribution of behaviors, passions, character traits, favoring or advising against certain behaviors. A large part of the critical culture of the twentieth century, from anthropology to philosophy, speaks to us of the social construction of gender in the case of human beings. That "sweetness" and "whim," "beauty" and "sensitivity" are "female qualities," as opposed to "strength" and naturally "courage," "rationality" and perhaps male "insensitivity," seem to us to be a peculiar ideological construction, the result of a power choice and also an obstinate instructive act which incessantly reproduces the ideology of gender in daily life, using film and stories, clothes and religious myths, family roles and visual stereotypes.

We never tire of discussing the degree of conventionality and the productivity of these distinctions. We are only interested that the language as a whole is the principle instrument of disclosure and a space of use, that is implementing the axis of gender opposition as a fundamental metaphor for understanding and describing much of the world. The gender of the word subtly influences our perception of the object, even though we know perfectly well that this is a purely external and grammatical feature.

And here we discover a new aspect of the naming game: what do we say when we give a typewriter a girl's name? We are evidently using a metaphor, we are attributing human qualities to the object and, in particular, those characteristics which our culture attributes to women: protective or capricious, pretty or sexy, jaunty or cheerful... Naturally, none of this should be taken too seriously: it is an attempt at jocular complicity, a form of seduction too erotic to be serious. And it should be remembered that there are feminine names for women's objects and names invented for masculine consumption—which leads to rather different effects of meaning.

And in any case , like the Adam of the religious myth or the platonic *nomothétes*, the inventor of feminine names for objects of use may be right. Because in our relationship with objects a part of our subconscious gender is expressed, that fetishism without which our world wouldn't be so full of commodities and the "sex appeal of the inorganic" (as Benjamin said of fashion objects). And therefore, by studying the feminine names of objects, perhaps we won't understand much of the things which surround us, but we will understand a great deal about ourselves and the complex and enveloping relationship which unites and contrasts the genders in our world.

When Objects
Have Women's Names

Silvana Annicchiarico
Curator of the Permanent Collection
of Italian Design at the Milan Triennale

The name is the archetype of the thing/
In the letters of rose there is the rose/
And the whole of the Nile in the word Nile.
Jorge Luis Borges

If we come across something without a name,
we invent one straightaway. And when we have
a good supply of names it seems
we are familiar with the world.
Andrea De Carlo, *Pura vita*

The problem of giving things names (choosing them, attributing them) makes up one of the decisive epistemological acts in all cultures of all civilizations. A name identifies and distinguishes. It confers identity and recognition. It separates an object from all the rest which belong to the same series, to a make or to the same family: it tells us for example that that chair and not just any old chair is the very one; that that lamp shouldn't be confused with all the other lamps that look like it; that that thing is what it is by virtue of the sign which, by naming it, distinguishes it.

Michel Foucault wrote in *Le Mots et les Choses* "The world is covered with blazons, characters, ciphers, obscure words, hieroglyphics."[1] It is the *signs* which make objects and artifacts legible, which allow each of us to organize our own cognitive map of the world. Design products too are covered by signs: proper names or trademarks, keys for recognition or ciphered codes. In any case, there is no "unsigned" object that does not turn to an identifying strategy of a nominalistic type to render itself perceivable, recognizable and classifiable. Jean Baudrillard put it well: "Dans notre économie fortement concurrentielle, peu de produits conservent longtemps une supériorité technique. Il faut leur donner des résonances qui les individualisent, les doter d'associations et d'images, leur donner des significations à de nombreux niveaux, si nous voulons qu'ils se vendent bien et suscitent des attachements affectifs."[2] The proper name is undoubtedly one of these *resonances*. Perhaps the first: the most immediate, the most evident.

The fact that often (but not always, as we will see more clearly later on) designers or design historians have underestimated the importance of names attributed to things is only an attempt to exorcise a problem which is, however, unavoidable and central. We could formulate it in this way: the name of an object is legitimately part of the project which generated it. Even when it is attributed afterwards, like a false label, right but unnecessary, it ends by conditioning on some level the very nature of the object in question. If nothing else, because it influences its reception; because it orients—even on a subliminal level—the way in which the object is perceived; and because it conditions the use—individual or social—which a certain community decides to make of it.

Roland Barthes has definitively demonstrated the perceptive estrangement generated by the "names of Greek shepherds" (Polystyrene, Phenoplast, Polyethylene) attributed in turn to plastics.[3] And Umberto Eco, on his part, has invaluably demonstrated how every name is ontologically linked to the thing it designates.[4] Whether you like it or not, the name you give to an object cannot be dismissed as a secondary element or an accidental and non-essential accessory, unless you wish to rob the very object of its intrinsic sociality. Because it is first and foremost the name which makes an object a social entity: that is an identifiable artifact that can be read, sold and bought commercially (symbolically too) and traded by the community which decides to use it, to make it their own and to give it a *value*. Mauro Ferraresi and Fulvio Carmagnola perceptively wrote: "It is the name which invites the imagination to create myths, which tacks narrative elements onto commodities. It can be done negatively as art shows us, underlining its own lack and the impotence of words when faced with the queerness of the object, as the reaction to the disappointment of an "untitled" painting or as when you force yourself to find at least a theme, a topic, parallels which verbally accompany the thing you are faced with. Perhaps the name is not the archetype of the thing but it certainly helps to build its identity."[5]

In other words: the name is summary, promise and metaphor. It produces a creative re-framing of the named object. It is the first element in the interpretation of its identity. We all agree now that Picasso's *Guernica* would not be the same if it were called, for instance, *Transylvania*; or that Joyce's *Ulysses* would be largely something else were it entitled *Achilles* or *Diomedes*. Why should the same principle not apply to objects too? Why imagine that Marco Zanuso's armchair *Lady* or Ettore Sottsass's typewriter *Valentine* would be the same identical things were they called *Puppy* or *Rebecca*? Evidently this is not the case. Certainly, one of the examples mentioned (*Guernica*) is a unique piece, a work of art, while the design objects are mass-produced, in large numbers. But just like Joyce's *Ulysses* (or Hitchcock's *Vertigo*): the problem of giving mass-produced objects a name—whether functional or cultural is of little matter—is one of modernity's great challenges.

It hasn't always been this way. Between the end of the 1800's and the beginning of the 1900's objects—handmade and industrial—did not yet have a proper name, limiting themselves to a common noun which provided a typological, morphological, functional or decorative description: in 1898 for example, a great cabinet-maker like Carlo Bugatti made "a small sofa in vellum" while in 1905 Richard Ginori proposed his luxury "chamber porcelain services." Sometimes codes took the place of names: at the Turin Exposition in 1911 Olivetti's typewriter appeared with the name *M1*, while between 1912 and 1915 Fiat designed the first prototype of a mass-produced small car with the name *Fiat Zero*.[6] Between the wars the approach began to change beginning in the transport sector: motorcycles and automobiles were the first mass-produced products to be "baptized" with a proper name (Fiat launched *Barilla* in 1932 and *Topolino* in 1943, Moto Guzzi produced *Alce* in 1939, *Cicogna* and *Airone* in 1940).

However, it was only from the end of the Second World War, and especially from the years of the economic boom, that companies began to systematically address the problem of what to call objects. First they did it functionally, then—increasingly—emotionally. While ordinary names too become more precise and polished, as proved for example by the *A-lessico* recently compiled by Alessi to define a typological vocabulary shared by the company group (designers, technician, salespeople, users), proper names shrug off a flatly denotative relationship with the product and place themselves in that intermediate area of experience which lies between the conception of the project and the perception of the object.

The proper name should certainly not be mistaken with the brand or the logo. The brand is often patronymic (Gucci, Alessi), the logo (Kodak, Sony, Nike) is esoteric and allusive. Both evoke a "guarantee of belonging"[7] or a group of phono-symbolical suggestions which may be highly refined but unable to connote the identity of the single object. The name is different. The proper name participates and contributes to the narration of the object which bears it. It transforms it into a tale. It gives information about its origins on the map of the imaginary. It communicates something about the social, economic and cultural condition not only of the those who designed and made it but also of those who elect to use it. Like actual naming (which emerged in Italy between the fourth and fifth century, in that phase in which the affirmation of Christianity led to a strong recognition of the value of individual identity), the naming of objects is determined by the merging of countless voices from the most disparate sources: personal memories, affective transactions, family traditions, but also answers or allusions or suggestions which come from literature, mythology and, lately, from the world of show-business, mass communication and TV. Whatever its genesis, the name creates a "halo" around the object. It interweaves networks of possible extensions of its meaning. It is simultaneously able to evoke and connote. At times it is born as a conscious semantic loan, almost a sort of program which concentrates the design intentions and strategies which have generated it; at other times, instead, it is more cryptic and remains further from the immediacy of the thing. But between the two possible opposite poles of nomination—that of meaninglessness, sheer arbitrariness and that of flat denomination (as in the case of MacIntosh's Apple, chosen because "it is the name of a kind of apple")—the name works. It works and makes the imagination work. Ferraresi and Carmagnola write: "If the object were, so to speak, perfectly transparent, without mysteries, without questions, if its name were totally explicative, declarative, denotative, the web of meaning would close too soon, and the dynamic of desire would be mutilated. The name is one of those instances, those devices, whose task is to keep this virtual narrative space open, far beyond the strategic and functional requirements of branding."[8] Thus it is precisely here, in the space which separates and unites the name of the thing that the object releases the most meaning possible. Or meanings, plural. It is this that we should explore and work on.

Many objects belonging to post-war Italian design have a woman's name. A preliminary census, without claiming to be exhaustive, but aiming to at least fence off a coherent semantic field and identify a widespread marketing strategy, led us to locate almost two hundred:[9] far more than the number of objects with male names shown in company catalogues. Designers, when questioned about the causes of this predilection, mostly reply citing different reasons: one of the "statistic-quantitative" type and the other of the "emotional" type. Paolo Rizzatto (designer of objects with allusive names such as *Lola, Titania, Costanza* and

Berenice) for example asserts: "I believe that names of objects are more often female than male for two reasons. The first is that male designers are numerically predominant compared to female designers. The second is that creating an object is a little like conceiving a creature: you end up growing fond of it, and you call it with a woman's name because it inspires you with feelings of tenderness, protection and intimacy."[10] It is something like Italo Calvino's *Invisible Cities*, marked by a female identity which the tales of Marco Polo and Kublai Khan evoke and suggest above all with their names (Fedora, Isaura, Smeraldina and so on).[11] Many Italian design objects too make their mark in the Babel of commodities wrapped in an atmosphere of gynaeceum emanating precisely and chiefly from the fact of having a woman's name.

Of course *Costanza* or *Berenice*, *Gilda* or *Sabrina* bear women's names, but they are not women. They are lamps, chairs, armchairs. But, as we said, it is precisely here, in the space which remains open between sign and thing, in the opaque fissure which opens between the name and the object, that the imagination can go to work. Here (here *too*) objects become—to quote Bruno Latour—a cross between "artifacts" and "fetishes," between technological body and point of attraction of psychological and cultural tensions.[12] The re-semanticism worked by the female name envelops, that is, the functional structure of the object and contributes to reconfirming it "in its value as a commodity at the very moment in which you subtract it from its immediate utility in order to re-launch it into the sphere of the symbolic."[13] Together with tangible forms and performable functions then, the name attributed to an object also contributes to personify—

above all in the case of *a name of a female person*—a communicative and representative order which conveys and concentrates in mass-produced products a range which is extremely rich in possible relations and narratives.

There are interesting stories behind the ways and the procedures of choosing a name: stories which enrich with new hues our knowledge of working methods and methods of elaborating a design project on the part of many designers and companies. Together with the stories there are many tactics and strategies for naming which deserve to be analyzed. These range from casual, nominal and arbitrary attributions, perhaps decided by the marketing chief of the manufacturing firm merely to meet classification and catalogue requirements, to names proposed by the designers themselves with the intention of paying homage to the muses which inspired them, to recall a particularly dear female presence[14] or to transfer to the designed object their own world of affections, friendships and loves. Other times the choice derives from precise morphological analogies between the object and the name which is attributed to it (with its sinuous curves and rounded shapes Gaetano Pesce's *Donna* armchair evokes the archetype of the buxom female silhouette in the Italian male's imagination) or by a deliberate and conscious indication of style (Marco Zanuso's *Lady* armchair's elegant contours, colors and materials recall an idea of refinement and "nobility" which the name renders explicit and accentuates).

Then there are names which acknowledge an extraction, an origin, or an elective affinity (Enzo Mari calls a chair which alludes to the *Thonet* archetype *Tonietta* and chooses instead a widely diffused name like *Teresa* for another chair which has more markedly popular formal traits) and those which derive from an "image" choice operated by the manufacturers. For example, *Artemide*, after taking the name of the God of Light, for many years decided to call all its lamps by mythological names (*Arianna, Dafne, Ebe, Diana, Giunone, Elettra)* and has only recently chosen to update its advertising strategy adopting short international names like *e-light* and *Sui* which, due to their greater proximity to the logic of the logo, position themselves better in the global market. Finally there are names which forcefully enter merchandising in the contemporary imagination, opening links or affective routes which enrich the object's "cultural" value of use: Paolo Rizzatto's *Lola* is therefore a homage to Marlene Dietrich and her legs, Sergio Asti's *Zelda* evokes the homonymous character of Scott Fitzgerald's *Tender is the Night* and the spirit of the roaring Twenties, Gastone Rinaldi's *Sabrina* aspires, starting with its very name, to be as spirited and impertinent as Audrey Hepburn's character in Billy Wilder's film, while Carlo Mollino's *Gilda* is an evident homage to Rita Hayworth's sensuality.

On a more rigorously semantic level, we may identify four great macro-groups which represent and synthesize to some extent all the female taxonomies of Italian design objects:

— objects given prescribed female epithets, that is, those collective common nouns which language uses to evoke femininity in all its different, possible declinations (*Donna, Lady, Bambola, Mami*, etc.);

— objects denominated with women's proper names drawn from the catalogue of national and international names (*Carlotta, Elda, Chiara, Isetta*, etc.);

— objects overloaded with cultural echoes choosing for themselves the name of *celebrated women in literature* (*Berenice, Fedra, Zelda*) or *mythology* (*Dafne, Arianna,* etc.);

— finally, objects which allude to divas or show-business personalities, be it to exploit a trend, to offer itself as an echo or replica of a successful "fetish" or to indicate a kind of underground linguistic and cultural affinity (*Barbarella, Gilda, Lola,* etc.).

This type of naming is obviously not alien to the spirit of the times: the diagram of names is also affected, in its own way, by the zeitgeist. In the past, as we have seen, many Italian companies (Kartell, Rima) held names to be of little importance, using ciphered codes or ordinary denotative names in the firm belief that the object counted above all for its functional value of use: between 1950 and 1970 in the Kartell catalogue, for example, there are some rare sporadic examples of products which have a name, sometimes by virtue of the fact that the name and the object clearly resemble each other (*Ragno* [Spider], *Cento Piedi* [Centipede]), at other times due to an onomatopoeic type link (*Tic Tac*).[15] In the Fifties and Sixties, however, companies could still quietly draw upon the national-popular names and choose to call a bicycle *Graziella* or a sewing machine *Mirella* in the sound belief that these names meant an *analogon* (or an immediately identified temptation) to the housewives who would use the object in question. Today, in the era of the global market, almost no object can call itself like that any more. The logic of the logo imposes pleasant-sounding, short proper names, easily understood in different languages.

The more *friendly* objects become, the more important it is that the name they are given should evoke an idea of familiarity, friendship, affinity. Or the atmosphere of a game, allusion and irony, as happens with the whimsical and bizarre female names which a designer attentive to matters of naming like Philippe Starck loves to give his objects (*Miss C.O.C.O, ERO/S/*). Which are now all—to use a famous definition of Winnicot—*transitional objects*.[16] They allow meaning to transit, they do not consume it. And they can do this thanks also to the network of relationships which the name manages to weave around itself, beginning with their naked evidence of things.

The exhibition *I'm No Lady* does not mean therefore to be a simple show of objects. It means to display, rather, objects and names. That is, objects and *signs* which lead the very object to make itself in part *different*. Or, in any case, to open itself to the *other*. Its ambition is, starting with objects, to evoke the world (or the imagination) that objects involve and move. The real theme of the exhibition is neither the objects nor their names, but the relationship which ties them: a relationship which it is impossible to display but only suggest, evoke and hypothesize, so that it is the visitor who closes the circuit with his emotional and cognitive syntheses. *I'm No Lady* means to be, therefore and above all, an occasion for reflecting on the relationship which ties us to objects. On the use we have made of them or that we could have made of them. And on those symbolic and cultural processes which have led certain objects to become a definitive part of the things of life. Ours and everybody else's.

Note

1. Michel Foucault, *Les mots et les choses,* Gallimard, Paris, 1966.

2. Jean Baudrillard, *Le système des objets,* Gallimard, Paris, 1968, p. 262: "In our strongly competitive economy, few products preserve their technical supremacy for very long. It is necessary to attribute them with a resonance that make them stand out, endow them with associations and images, give them meanings on different levels, if we want them to sell well and arouse affective relations."

3. Roland Barthes, *Mythologies,* Editions du Seuil, Paris, 1957.

4. Umberto Eco, *Il nome della rosa,* Bompiani, Milan, 1980.

5. Mauro Ferraresi and Fulvio Carmagnola, *Merci di culto. Ipermerce e società mediale,* Castelvecchi, Rome, 1999, p. 68.

6. For all these details, cf. Vittorio Gregotti, *Il disegno del prodotto industriale. Italia 1860-1980*, Electa, Milan, 1982.

7. Valeria Bucchetti, *La messa in scena del prodotto. Packaging: identità e consumo*, Franco Angeli Editore, Milan, 1999, p. 65.

8. Mauro Ferraresi and Fulvio Carmagnola, op. cit., p. 71.

9. Cf. the index published in the appendix of this volume.

10. Interview granted to the author in December 2001.

11. Italo Calvino, *Le città invisibili,* Einaudi, Turin, 1972.

12. Bruno Latour, *Facts, Artifacts, Fetishes – A Reflection on Techniques*, 1996.

13. Maurizio Vitta, *Il progetto della bellezza. Il design fra arte e tecnica, 1851-2001*, Finaudi, Turin, 2001, p. 313.

14. Alessandro Mendini says for example: "I think that an object I design should be a person's friend—pleasant, affectionate and faithful. In spite of this I always find it immensely hard to find a name for it. The name should be simple and charming, but it should also express an intention, a theory. It is a defining moment in the life of a project. In the case of the Spanish rug I called *Christina*, the idea was to dedicate it to the person who, with infinite patience, had designed and worked on it to the end, who knew it almost better than I did, the tiniest details of its decoration, technique, colors. I mean the designer Maria Christina Hamel, who was my chief partner at that time and who now has a studio in Milan. The demonstration is the homage for a job done in tandem." Declaration made to the author, January 2002.

15. The founder of Kartell Giulio Castelli says: "In the post-war period our conception was functional not decorative. We were against giving fantasy names to objects. The housewife who went into a shop didn't buy a name or a code but a 30cm diameter bucket or a wash-tub with handles. On the other hand we were the first to bring in data-processing in order to register all objects. So it was natural to call the objects themselves by numbers, with codes. And the initial number changed according to the technology and material used (polyethylene had one number, polypropylene had another). Certainly, I now realize that it might have been better for the public to have a name. But we manufactured household articles. And how can you give a name to a carafe, a plate-rack, a glass? And lamps? And furnishings? Things changed in the Eighties..." Interview granted to the author on 17 November 2001.

16. Cf. Donald Woods Winnicott, *Gioco e realtà*, Armando Editore, Rome, 1974.

Female Epithets

Themes and variations by Piero Fornasetti, 1964. 500 variants on the same subject have been created: the face of a woman, Lina Cavalieri, who the designer found in a nineteenth-century French magazine. The face embodies all the characteristics of the classic female archetype.

Alongside objects which bear the name of a woman, Italian design presents some objects which simply carry the name "woman" itself, or a variation of it. Or more precisely: one of the many epithets with which language evokes and designates the very idea of femininity. *Donna, Lady, Bambola, Diva, Miss, Mami*: in a world saturated with signs and cluttered with names, it is precisely epithets such as these, apparently impersonal but actually loaded with affective, enunciative or relational implications, which advance precise and significant modalities of use.

Donna, aspiring to antonomasia ("donna" means "woman" in Italian), offers itself as a paradigmatic and morphological mimesis of femininity. *Lady* suggests a fruition marked by composed and refined elegance. *Diva* plays on a promise of the mirror refraction of identity. *Miss Sissi* oscillates between mischievous discretion and allusive quotation. *Mami* immerses the object in an inevitably domestic, family and childlike focus. As for *Bambole* ("dolls" in Italian), the epithet recalls the most classic of female images, mixing it with the anomaly of a plural name used to indicate a singular object. But it is precisely here, in this ambiguity of meaning, that the magic of naming lies. Indicating perhaps that the world of objects like the world of women is always and in any case a plural world.

Lady

Armchair
Marco Zanuso
1951
Arflex

Innovative from both the technological point of view
and the point of view of production methods (it uses
foam rubber instead of the traditional upholsterer's
padding, and puts four individual pieces—sides, seat
and back—together to make a whole like an
assembly line), *Lady's* sober elegance recalls
bourgeois chairs.

The name betrays Zanuso and Arflex's ambition to
make it the "madam" of bourgeois salons in Italy in
the early Fifties.

The advertising photograph printed suggests a use
tinged by an idea of abandon in which symbols of
elegance (black gloves, silk scarf and string of pearls)
coexist with the privacy guaranteed by the
penumbra.

Milan Triennale Collection

Using injection polyurethane foam in an innovative way, Gaetano Pesce made an armchair with sinuous and sensual lines for B&B whose evident anthropomorphism alludes to a prehistoric goddess of fertility and recalls the buxom curves of the female body.

Almost a remake of Anita Ekberg's torso made into an armchair: soft, inviting, generous.

The quintessence of femininity transformed into object, part mother, part lover. The name *Donna* ("woman" in English) oscillates between semantic excess and erotic mischief.

Donna

Armchair
Gaetano Pesce
1969
B&B

Milan Triennale Collection

My job is to give
a shape to the values
of joy, sexuality, a certain
type of religiosity,
the coexistence
of different philosophical
values, typical of being
female.
The masculine world
is a monolithic world
which has a repetitive
conception of life,
with identical behaviors,
while female life is at
once a multidisciplinary
life: being a mother,
being a wife, being
a worker, means that
this female world
squarely expresses this
multidisciplinary age.
(Gaetano Pesce, *Modo*,
n. 205)

Le Bambole

Armchair
Mario Bellini
1972
B&B

Le Bambole *is like a rag doll fashioned severely and clothed expertly: like a living organism in a balanced symbiosis between inside and out.*
(Mario Bellini)

First produced in 1972, *Le Bambole* immediately created a stir and interest, along with the barbs of criticism which stung the advertising launch campaign conceived by photographer Oliviero Toscani: a sequence of photographs in which the model Donna Jordan, naked from the waist up, tempts: "Shall we meet to talk?" "About what?" "Heck, about *Bambole*!"

Milan Triennale Collection

Diva

Mirror
Ettore Sottsass
1984
Memphis

Every "diva" is a *star*. A star who lives in reflected
light. Calling the mirror he designed for Memphis
Diva, Sottsass finds the essence of being a diva in the
theme of reflection and works his poetics of "talking
surfaces" on the object. The mirror speaks: with its
star shape (a true star) and with its act of reflecting, it
implies a metaphor on the purposeful narcissism
which dominates show-business society.

*...any form is always
metaphorical, never totally
metaphysical; never a
"destiny," always a fact
which somehow has
historical references which
can anyway be extracted.*
Ettore Sottsass, 1993,
(in *Ettore Sottsass,
Cosmit '99*, p. 90)

Memphis Collection

Miss Sissi

Lamp
Philippe Starck
1990
Flos

Made in colored techno-polymers, *Miss Sissi* is the plastic imitation of a fabric lampshade: a design object which summons up pop-culture forms and valences from the historical memory.
Slender and graceful, its name evokes the character of Princess Sissi played on the silver screen by a delightful Romy Schneider, in a popular series of films characterized by a palette of flamboyant colors. Just like the colors Starck and Flos attribute to this *mignon* lamp: the "miss" of modern lampshades, with a regal destiny (or vocation) inscribed in its name.

Milan Triennale Collection

Mami

Pots
Stefano Giovannoni
1999
Alessi

The curved and rounded shape of this series of pots
evokes the memory of an old-country kitchen or the
shape of vases and jars of ancient traditional cultures.
The name Mami sums up this idea of genuineness, of
domestic familiarity, and projects onto the object that
"poetics of affections" which is typical of the designer.

*With Mami I tried to rediscover the pot we all have in
our memory and imaginary. Mami is the pot I observed
from below when I was a child, steaming on the rings
of the cooker. It is grandmother's pot.*
(Stefano Giovannoni in the video *Mr. Giovannoni and
His Creatures, Metamorphoses*, 2001)

Alessi Collection

Ordinary Women's Proper Names

Women's proper names. Ordinary names: names of women who have the names of women in everyday life. Names of wives and daughters, secretaries and friends: Muses, companions. Women who leave a sign of their presence on the design procedure which leads to the making of an object letting their proper name transit through the object itself. As an inscription. As a thank-you. As proof of affection and recognition.

There are those who, by using their names, pay homage to their wives (*Genni* by Gabriele Mucchi, *Irma* by Achille Castiglioni), their secretaries

(*Luisa* by Franco Albini), a cherished friend (*Anna G.* by Alessandro Mendini). There are those who summarize in the name the tender joy of their daughter (*Gaia* by Carlo Bartoli), those who allude to Mozart's wife (*Costanza* by Paolo Rizzatto) or Le Corbusier's collaborator (*Charlotte* by Sergio Asti) and those who attribute to a lamp (*Chiara* by Mario Bellini) not just the chief quality of the light it produces but also the shape of the female figure (a nun) which inspired it. In an act of naming loaded with allusions, reminiscences and memories, the design objects which exhibit women's proper names make up a varied but coherent whole. And remind us how much the world and the practice of design fails to keep itself alien or immune to the logic of emotion and affectivity.

Genni

Chaise longue
Gabriele Mucchi
1935 production Pino
1982 Zanotta

A manifestly rationalist design, *Genni* has a chrome-steel frame and an adjustable seat which can be used in two positions. Gabriele Mucchi has given it the name of his first wife. Another of Mucchi's chairs, *Susanna*, has the name of the designer's second wife.

Compared to objects of the same typology produced by rationalist design in its "heroic" period, Genni *stands out due to the greater focus on comfort, a considerable formal simplification and, at the same time, a strong expressive and architectonic charge.*
(Stefano Casciani, *Mobili come architetture*, Arcadia Edizioni, 1984, p. 26)

As for propaganda, my explicit desire, or rather condition, is that only the name Mucchi be used and not Architect Mucchi. Architects make architecture (and I have made some), not chairs. Chairs are perhaps made by designers. But I am not a designer, I am only, with kindest regards, your Mucchi.
(Letter from Gabriele Mucchi to Aurelio Zanotta, December 1981, for the study of the reissue of the chaise longue)

Zanotta Collection

Fenis

Chair
Carlo Mollino
1947
1985 Zanotta

Is it a woman's name? The name of an animal? Is it only something whispered?
Certainly with *Fenis* we are faced with an object which undisputedly evokes sensuality, eroticism, sinuosity. Applying his famous curvy lines to a morphologically ambiguous object, Carlo Mollino insinuates his fascination with femininity in the carved beech of this chair which seems unable to live were it not "inhabited" by the women Mollino himself photographs sitting on it. The polysemy of the name, in this case, does not hide the womanly aspect, but immerses it in an atmosphere loaded with sensual languor.

Maria Luisa Ballabio Collection

Luisa

Chair
Franco Albini
1950
Poggi

A rare example of compositional rationality united with the elegance of formal solutions, *Luisa* presents an only apparent simplicity: the purity which you can deduce from the discontinuity of the parts is an expression of preferential treatment given to the joints and the points of connection. The seat and the back are fixed so that they allow the plywood to conserve its natural flexibility, and they adapt to the form and position of the body.
The name is a dedication to Mrs. Luisa Colombini (Gino Colombini's wife), Franco Albini's personal secretary for over twenty years.

Milan Triennale Collection

Fiorenza

Armchair
Franco Albini
1952
Arflex

Conceived as a reworking of a design for an armchair
which Franco Albini had designed in 1939 and from
which very few models were handcrafted, the name
Fiorenza reveals its aristocratic leanings and ambition
to occupy a place of excellence among the furniture of
bourgeois salons in the Italy of post-war
reconstruction. With its spare but not bloodless lines,
Fiorenza invites the user to assume a correct posture
for conversing, relaxing and reading. Although
indebted to the typology of traditional *bergères*, it
presents very modern formal elements which increase
the suggestion of its decorum and elegant sobriety.

Milan Triennale Collection

Auretta

Hairdryer
Alberto Rosselli
Tito Angelo Anselmi
1956
CGE

At least two thirds of the more than 130 models of hairdryers on sale in Italy around the mid-Fifties were based on a design which foresaw the pistol grip. *Auretta* was born of the desire to suppress this stereotype without forcing the user's wrist and hand to perform painful acrobatics. This is why Rosselli and Anselmi, sensitive to the teachings of the ULM school and an extremely severe and functional design, encapsulate the hairdryer mechanism in an easy to hold cylinder closed simply at each end by two snap-open covers.

The name, in this case, attenuates the object's austerity, rendering it more intimate and familiar: the word aura (air, breeze, light wind) produced by the hairdryer becomes, in the form of an endearment, the proper name of the object which produces it.

Milan Triennale Collection

Mirella

Sewing machine
Marcello Nizzoli
1957
Necchi

"Making machines which do not require women to ask for help from an engineer or technician to make them work." This is the claim Necchi used in the second half of the Fifties to launch a simple and economical sewing machine whose ambition was to mechanize women's housework aiming at a voluminous and widespread distribution.

The choice of the name *Mirella* (from Latin *mirari*, beautiful, to be admired), widely used at that time, above all among working class women, turns out to be particularly apt: it exorcises the fatigue of working, making it aesthetic and immersing the object in a dreamlike aura emphasized by the advertising campaign.

The demonstrators, girls who go here and there, from home to home, to show, explain and persuade people to purchase a machine are a Necchi invention. Competitions like Bride of Italy *(the prize went to the Italian woman who could prove she possessed the most homemaking virtues and spirit of self-sacrifice) produced excellent promotional and advertising results.*
(Corrado Pizzinelli, *Vittorio Necchi e la sua industria d'avanguardia* in *Costume*, A. III, n. 18-19, 1958)

Milan Triennale Collection

Graziella

Bicycle
Technical Dept
1963
Carnielli

Practical, light and easy to handle, with small 16cm-diameter wheels compared to the 60-70 cm wheels of traditional models, and furthermore collapsible for easy transport (for example in a car trunk) and storage in narrow spaces, in a short space of time *Graziella* becomes one of the best-selling models of bicycles in Italy in the early Sixties. Its users are above all women required and permitted by the euphoric atmosphere of the economic boom to move more rapidly in a space adjacent to the domestic environment or the workplace.

Like the *Mirella* sewing machine in the Fifties, the bicycle manufactured by the Canielli Technical Dept. also chooses a name which is simultaneously working class but also loaded with cultured resonance (*Graziella* derives from the Latin name of the imperial age which means "graceful, pleasant, winsome," but is a fundamentally Christian name because it is connected to Divine Grace).

Despite its apparent simplicity, it is an almost surrealist object (Salvador Dalí had his photograph taken holding a *Graziella*).

At the time advertising launched it as Brigitte Bardot's Rolls Royce.

Bottecchia Cicli srl Collection

Gaia

Chair
Carlo Bartoli
1967
Arflex

*When I made it, with this super shiny body like a car,
there was a tin can in my workshop containing red
paint. My daughter Anna, who was very small then,
took the tin can and a brush and started to paint the
seat. It was a gesture that expressed such gaiety and
cheerfulness that I decided to call the chair Gaia. With
Masera we then based the whole advertising
campaign on these pictures of Anna painting Gaia,
of course.*
(Carlo Bartoli, December 2001)

Milan Triennale Collection

Chiara

Lamp
Mario Bellini
1967
Flos

Flos Collection

Made from a sheet of inox steel cut and folded to form both the base and the diffuser, the lamp designed by Bellini for Flos is an emblematic example of congruency between name and thing: not just due to the reasons pronounced by the designer himself in his statement printed here, but also because the same etymology connects the adjective *clarus/a* to an idea of luminosity.

The picture of the nun printed on the opposite page is the one Bellini produced whenever he was invited to illustrate the object's genesis.

There is no base, no stem, no head; if you look deep down inside it is empty, it is just full of light; if you lift it, it is as light as a leaf and you feel that its form is a certain balance of elastic tensions easily alterable by the mere pressure of the hand.

From the beginning we connected a charming though not "rational" image with this lamp: a nun with one of those beautiful, wobbling starched linen hats, vanishing and becoming light and habit; so in the studio we always called it "the nun" until we found this name Chiara *which, though conserving part of that suggestion, seemed to me to be more appropriate for this clear and simple idea.*

(Mario Bellini, *Ottagono*, n. 11, October 1968)

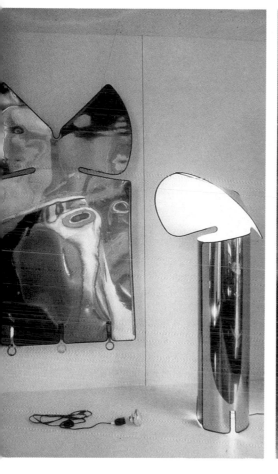

Carlotta

Armchair
Afra and Tobia Scarpa
1967
Cassina

Continuing their work on the theme of padding, which in 1960 had already produced the *Bastiano* sofa for Gavina (and in 1968 had generated *Coronado* for C&B, the first industrially manufactured modular living room drowning every structural metallic part in soft polyurethane), in 1967 Afra and Tobia Scarpa design a flamboyantly colored knockdown armchair for Cassina which appropriates the taste for bright colors typical of the contemporary "hippie" culture (but which is also a precursor of the use of color which will be typical of Benetton, with whom the two designers have worked at length).

The choice of the name is almost always suggested by the designer who presents it to the company with possible alternatives, subject to a check on its originality within the sphere of the same commodity sector.
*The name is therefore part of the design procedure and connected to the elements which suggest and evoke the design (*La Rotonda: *the archetypes of architecture as desire to get back to traditional typologies) and sometimes its material (*I Feltri: *a name as synonym of the material). As far as those products which have a woman's name are concerned, perhaps the name recalls and pays homage to the Muse which inspires the designer.*
(Franco Cassina, 17 December 2001)

Cassina Collection

Charlotte

Small armchair
Sergio Asti
1968
Zanotta

I have always thought carefully about the names of my objects. Zelda, the armchair for Poltronova, refers to the Scott Fitzgerald character in Tender is the Night. *Luigiona, a glass vase for Seguso, is the nickname I use for my wife: she is called Mariangela, but I affectionately call her Luigiona. Tomoko, the lamp I designed for I Tre, is a homage to a beautiful girl who came to the studio and helped me with the project. The lamp* Inao *alludes to my loyal collaborator.*

Alice is a name I use when I have to design something particularly fantastic, susceptible to surges of emotion or bursts of imagination. I proposed it for a vase for Salviati and for a table for UP&UP. Obviously the reference is to the character created by Lewis Carroll in Alice in Wonderland, *which has been my favourite fairy tale since I was a very small child.*

Finally Charlotte *is a homage to Charlotte Perriand, Le Corbusier's colleague and collaborator from 1927 to 1937, head of interior design and furnishings. With Le Corbusier and Pierre Jeanneret she worked on some of the most prestigious objects of* Équipement *in the Twenties. With my chair I picked up on their use of a curved chrome tube, inspired by the Bauhaus movement.*

(Sergio Asti, December 2001)

Zanotta Collection

61

Bicia

Armchair
Carlo Bartoli
1969
Arflex

With its molded fiberglass body, Bicia is an armchair which should be seen above all in profile in order to appreciate the ergonomic line with which it invites and welcomes a female body harmoniously integrating itself with the anatomical posture in the act of sitting.

When I design, while I design and make the model, I start to conceive of it and call it by a name. Perhaps it is temporary, because it is then debated by the company, but I need to personify the object I am working on straightaway. Names influence the fortune of objects, on the market too. What is important is that they should remain in your memory and strike you in the same way as the form of the objects do. For example, I believe that a disyllabic name is easier to remember. That is why I chose Bi-cia or Ga-ia as names for two of my armchairs. Armchairs are definitely female objects. It is logical therefore that they be given women's names. I think they are more beautiful seen from behind or in profile, even when they are "inhabited."
(Carlo Bartoli, December 2001)

Arflex Collection

Alessia

Chair
Giotto Stoppino
1970
Driade

Steel-tube supporting frame, body-in-glass resin.
A form which transmits the idea of a surge and push
upwards. An emblematic example of research into
plastic materials which characterizes a large part of
Italian design beginning in the second-half of the
Sixties. The name, like other products produced for
Driade in that decade, has Greek roots: from the verb
aléxein (to defend, protect) *aléxia* means "defender,"
"protector."

*Driade, a name deriving from the Greek, initially used
to attribute Greek names to its products, like the case
of Giotto Stoppino's chair. Then it was the turn of the
designers, beginning with Philippe Starck, to baptize
the objects. For example, the* Ubik *collection used the
names of characters from Philip K. Dick's science
fiction novel, taking its cue from urban youth culture.
Driade's* Aleph *on the other hand takes its inspiration
from Jorge Luis Borges' story of the same name.*
(Luisa Acerbi, December 2001)

Driade Collection

63

Giona

Lamp
Giorgina Castiglioni
1973
Bilumen

The name of this adjustable
ABS resin lamp with its
diffuser in opal white
cellidor does not allude to
the biblical prophet, famous
for ending up in the belly of
a whale, but is born of the
syncopation of the designer's
own name, who in this way
expresses, though in a
contracted and slightly
masked form, the dream of
many creators: that of giving
their own name to the product
of their work. The name as
autobiographical trace.

Milan Triennale Collection

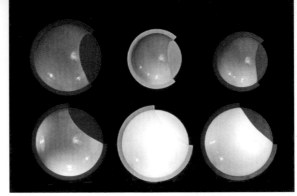

Gio(rgi)na Castiglioni

Celestina

Chair
Marco Zanuso
1978
Zanotta

Though the word "celestino" in Italian means pale-blue,
this name choice has nothing to do with the color.
Celestina by Zanotta is produced in various colors
(black, white, Russian red, natural leather), all very
dissimilar to sky blue, baby blue and blue. The name
therefore derives from a different semantic field to the
one of color: perhaps in its rustic and unaffected
grace, it evokes the charm of an object which is so
perfectly essential as to appear almost anonymous.
Or common, universal. Like a country girl, an ordinary
girl, simple and direct, called upon to brighten
a bourgeois home of the late Seventies with her
old-fashioned charm.

Milan Triennale Collection

Irma

Chair
Achille Castiglioni
1979
Zanotta

Typologically similar to the solid wood chair *Lierna* which Castiglioni designed in 1960 taking inspiration from the model of a traditional Chinese chair, *Irma* is conceived as a classic chair to draw up to the dining table: the back, high and narrow, favors a decorous convivial position and facilitates the movements of whoever has to serve lunch or pass the dishes to the other diners.

The name is a homage to the designer's wife: almost an affectionate allusion to their domestic intimacy, or a dedication to his inseparable dining (and life) companion.

Zanotta Collection

Tonietta

Chair
Enzo Mari
1981
Zanotta

With its die-cast aluminum frame, *Tonietta* is a revisit of *Thonet mod. 14*, the classic curved wooden chair made in 1859, almost an archetype in the history of design.

Thirty or forty years ago it was easier to find the "right" name for an object, a name corresponding to the specific characteristics of the design.
For example, I called one of my lighting systems Aggregato *because the name yielded the logic of the design, the possibility of aggregating different components.*
On another occasion I made a very simple bathroom accessory in bent iron and I called it Calvino.
Or I called an extremely minimal dinner service commissioned by Driade Minim. *In all these cases I used names which explained and implied the logic of the design.*
I had fun calling this chair Tonietta *because I realized it might have vaguely alluded to Thonet's archetype. It is certainly difficult to give a right name nowadays. It has to be agreeable, commercial, recognizable in the global market. There are few names nowadays which correspond precisely to designs....*
(Enzo Mari, December 2001)

Milan Triennale Collection

Lucrezia

Chair
Marco Zanini
1984
Memphis

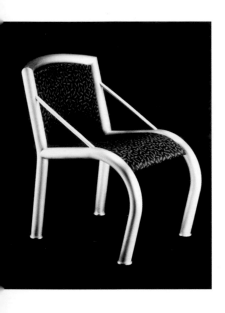

A typical example of Memphis style, Marco
Zanini's *Lucrezia* continues, from the radical
poetics of the group founded by Ettore Sottsass,
the taste for the surprising match of lines
(straight/curved) and materials (the aluminum
of the frame, the padded cotton fabric of the seat
and the back).

Like many other Memphis objects with women's
names (Massimo losa Ghini's chair *Juliette*
or Nathalie Du Pasquier's armchair *Denise*),
Lucrezia too is an allusive vehicle of emotions
and suggestions.

It can allude to Lucrezia Borgia's brazen sensuality,
but also to the dramatic Roman figure of Lucrezia
raped by Tarquinius, who inspired the French
playwright Jean Giraudoux to write his play *Pour
Lucrèce* (1953).

Roberto Gennari Collection

Costanza

Lamp
Paolo Rizzatto
1986
Luceplan

I called it Costanza *because it constitutes a constancy in the typology of lamps, the shade is a constant in time, a permanence of tradition. But Constance is also Mozart's wife, and for me Mozart's music is the most beautiful and appropriate for designing, cerebral and at the same time relaxing.*
Moreover, Costanza *is an old-fashioned name, but one which can still be used today. It is a recognizable name.*
(Paolo Rizzatto, December 2001)

Costanza is like a princess of the night.
Its soft light recalls Japanese rice-paper lamps.
(Maria Gabriella Formicola, *NEXT Strumenti per l'innovazione*, n. 9)

Luceplan Collection

An autograph letter from Mozart to his wife Constance.

Anna G.

Corkscrew
Alessandro Mendini
1994
Alessi

In this case the process of anthropomorphism comes not only with the naming but also with the ironic redesigning of a traditional object. The handle becomes a head with a bob hairstyle, the central piece has a retro look, the joints become shoulders from which slightly bent arms hang. The whole silhouette is composed and modest. But the advertising launch gives the object new meaning dressing it in the fluttering skirt of Marilyn in Billy Wilder's *The Seven Year Itch* (1955)

I wanted to obtain charm, grace and enigma through the face, the look, the smile and the body of this instrument destined to perform a small domestic ritual—a private, almost dancing ceremony. It was Alberto Alessi who realized that this face and this long body resembled the designer and artist Anna Gili, my dear friend.
I had unwittingly made a "design portrait," that is, a design inspired by the features of a real person.
Alberto said to me: "What if we called this corkscrew Anna G.?"
After this experience the theoretical problem of making objects with a face has led me to further study and elaboration.
In fact, today I am interested in making objects that can look at me with their eyes, objects that can see, that have a physiognomy, which see me as I see them.
(Alessandro Mendini, January 2002)

Alessi Collection

La Marie

Chair
Philippe Starck
1998
Kartell

Made from a single mold in transparent polycarbonate,
this chair of Starck's harks back to formal research
into the theme of the transparency of objects already
carried out by various international designers like
Erwine & Estelle Laverne (the Invisible Group objects,
including the chair *Champagne* in 1957), Giancarlo
Piretti (with his folding chair *Plia* of 1968) and above
all Shiro Kuramata, one of the chief representatives of
contemporary Japanese design (with his small
armchair *Miss Blanche*, from the name of the protagonist
of Tennessee Williams's *A Streetcar Called Desire*,
made in transparent acrylic resin with a decoration of
synthetic roses). Unlike all these projects which still
maintained some non-transparent structural element
(the pedestal, the frame, the legs), Starck aims for
total transparency and homogeneity of materials. In
this case the name chosen for the object is deliberately
ambivalent, it does not connote but implies: it might
allude to an apparition of the Virgin Mary, an
epiphany, but also social invisibility (or a tendency to
anonymity) of the most common woman's name.

Milan Triennale Collection

Figures from Mythology, History and Literature

At first glance, choosing to give a mass-produced object the name of unique creatures like the ones who populate mythological heavens or the pages of literature and history could seem a gesture of almost presumptuous glorification. Actually, this naming strategy represents an exemplary desire to immerse the object in a network of echoes and resonances which increase its symbolic and cultural value of use.

Calling a chair *Elettra* or a handle *Fedra* does not, in short, imply, on the part of designers and companies, any pretension to put their creatures on the same level as characters celebrated in the pages of Euripides or Sophocles (*Elettra*) or in the pages of Seneca or Racine (*Fedra*) but responds rather to a dual necessity, one of a commercial nature and the other of a cultural kind.

On the one hand names like *Cleopatra, Sherazade* or *Dalila* are sufficiently well-known and rooted in the collective consciousness to be easily remembered, memorized and reused through opportune displacements; on the other hand the apposition of similar names inevitably ends up giving the object a narrative and inviting the user to use it within a virtual narrative sequence. As though literature or mythology served to convey an object through a professedly diegetic scenario, not always apparent to a purely functional or exclusively formal evaluation. It is also by having names like these that objects offer themselves as plots of potential stories.

Medea

Chair
Vittorio Nobili
1954
Fratelli Tagliabue

From Earth to Myth. Actually from Brianza to Ancient Hellas. The name of this chair in curved plywood, designed by Vittorio Nobili and praised at the time by the likes of Gio Ponti, should originally have been called Meda, after the name of the small town in Lombardy where the manufacturer was based. The addition of a simple vowel—as Vittorio Nobili's family told us—generated the definitive name, linking the chair in question to the sorceress, the principal character in Euripides' homonymous tragedy (431 B.C.), who takes ferocious revenge on Jason who had betrayed her. A simple play on names? Not exactly. Whatever its origin, the name envelops the object in a mythical and solemn aura, in tune with the connotations of the figure of Medea beautifully rendered by the unforgettable performance given by Maria Callas in Pier Paolo Pasolini's film of the same name (1970).

Fratelli Tagliabue Collection

Elettra

Armchair
BPR
1954
Arflex

Private Collection

Faced with the formal severity and compositional economy of this armchair designed by BPR (Belgioioso, Peressutti, Rogers) for Arflex, the reminder of the figure of Electra (protagonist of one tragedy by Euripides and another by Sophocles, heroine of the vendetta which drives her brother Orestes to kill their mother Clitemnestra in order to punish her for the murder of their father Agamemnon) is above all a claim on classicism: like Electra, the armchair which carries her name wishes to remove itself from the fickleness of taste and the precariousness of fashions to find a design dimension of harmonious completeness and defined stability.

Selene

Chair
Vico Magistretti
1968
Artemide

Even among the designs of a rationalist designer like Vico Magistretti there are numerous and significant objects which have women's names: *Nathalie* the bed, *Elena* the small table, *Giunone* the lamp, *Charlotte* the chaise longue, *Sibilla* the door handle. In the case of the chair named *Selene*, a clear example of functional use of plastic materials in an innovative manner (where the "s" section of the legs means that the use of larger and heavier supporting frames can be avoided). The name is associated more with the company trademark than with the responsibility of the designer.

Sister of Flios, the Sun corresponding to the Moon in the Latin myth, Selene (represented by a young girl with a half-moon on her forehead, her head partly veiled, holding a burning torch) is, at a certain point, identical to the Greek figure of Artemis: as if by using a code name Ernesto Gismondi's company wished to transfer the idea of luminosity to an object which does not produce light.

Milan Triennale Collection

77

Frine

Lamp
Studio Tetrarch
1970
Artemide

From the name of the Greek courtesan Frine
(IV century B.C.), a synonym for prostitute
by antonomasia.
The Studio Tetrarch lamp, with a remote controlled
opening, parts like a flower, evoking one of the
gestures most loaded with sensuality. The allusion
is playful and amusing and the type of courtesan
it recalls has the natural spontaneity and attraction
of Shirley MacLaine in Billy Wilder's *Irma La Douce*
(1963).

Artemide Collection

Fedra

Door handle
Enrico Baleri
with Margherita de Mitri
1990
Kleis

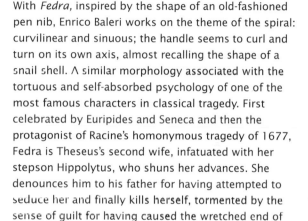

With *Fedra*, inspired by the shape of an old-fashioned pen nib, Enrico Baleri works on the theme of the spiral: curvilinear and sinuous; the handle seems to curl and turn on its own axis, almost recalling the shape of a snail shell. A similar morphology associated with the tortuous and self-absorbed psychology of one of the most famous characters in classical tragedy. First celebrated by Euripides and Seneca and then the protagonist of Racine's homonymous tragedy of 1677, Fedra is Theseus's second wife, infatuated with her stepson Hippolytus, who shuns her advances. She denounces him to his father for having attempted to seduce her and finally kills herself, tormented by the sense of guilt for having caused the wretched end of the young man who had rejected her. The basic transparency of the handle designed by Baleri seems to invite the eye to look beyond the object to reach the myth its name is linked to.

Milan Triennale Collection

Dalila

Chair
Gaetano Pesce
1980
Cassina

Pressed in rigid polyurethane but molded in such a way that it bypasses any idea of formal rigidity, *Dalila* epitomizes Gaetano Pesci's design poetics and his radical aversion to canons of modernist rationalism. Coherent with his idea of a "non repetitive series," according to which every sample produced must be slightly different from the others of the same series, due to the instability of the materials used or small formal details, with *Dalila* Pesci has made chairs with a vague and indefinite shape, all simultaneously alike and different from one another. Each time comparable to a bed of lava, a stone or a tree trunk, *Dalila* mocks the decoration of the bourgeois living room evoking a sort of archaic primitivism saturated in strength and power. The name alludes to the celebrated female figure of the Old Testament who seduced Samson, judge of Israel, cut his hair (in which the secret of his extraordinary strength was hidden) and gave it to the Philistines. In the same year, 1980, Pesci also designed a series of tables in synthetic resin for Cassina permitting a choice of the color and shape of the top called, precisely, *Sansone* (Samson).

Milan Triennale Collection

Berenice

Lamp
Paolo Rizzatto,
Alberto Meda
1985
Luceplan

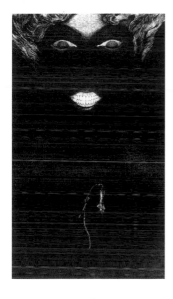

Made of a base, an articulated arm and a jointed head, *Berenice* is a low tension halogen lamp made up of 42 components in 13 different materials, a specific processing technology corresponding to each. The green of the glass reflector recalls antique brass table lamps and represents a mark of fondness for tradition in a lamp with a very innovative character.

In astronomy Berenice is a constellation made up of three stars plus a coma of small stars. The lamp is made just so: it has three points of articulation and describes the constellation perfectly.
But Berenice is also the name of a character and the title of a tale by Edgar Allan Poe.
It is an outmoded name which leaves an impression and which can be pronounced in every language. I am always attentive to this aspect when I choose a name for my object.
(Paolo Rizzatto, December 2001)

Milan Triennale Collection

Olimpia

Lamp
Carlo Forcolini
1986
Artemide

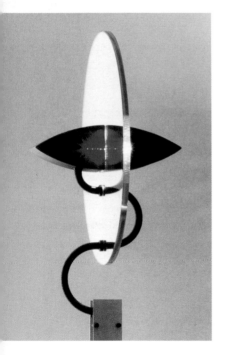

A circle of tempered glass cuts a source of light which has the shape of an eye. Or, vice versa, a bright, artificial eye is embedded in a transparent disc. Playing with the co-penetration of curvilinear geometrical shapes, Carlo Forcolini engenders a lamp which has the severity of an abstract composition and the charm of a dream-like vision. The female name in this case, confers upon the object an extraordinarily cultural added value: whether it be an Olympian Greek goddess or the heroine Ariosto celebrated in *Orlando Furioso*, the name given to the object is a sort of invitation to begin spinning a potential tale. Almost a transparent *Invitation au voyage*.

Surrealist artist Magritte painted this analogy of sun and the eye in one of his most disturbing paintings, and in his famous film Le Chien Andalou *Spanish director Bunuel cuts an eye with a razor. Two representations of the eye with opposite meanings: in the first the symbol is restored to its original meanings, in the second the symbol is desecrated. In conceiving this lamp for Artemide I was certainly more inspired by Bunuel.*
(Carlo Forcolini, *Carlo Forcolini. Immaginare le cose*, Electa, Milan, 1990, p. 67)

Carlo Forcolini Collection

82

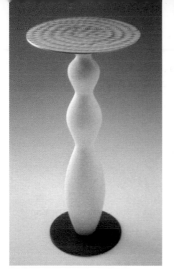

Cleopatra

Small table
Marco Zanuso Jr.
1987
Memphis

An ironic, allusive, mischievous but also prescriptive name. Adopting the name of the most famous Queen of ancient Egypt, the small wooden and metal table designed by Marco Zanuso Jr. for Memphis plays with an icon rooted in the popular imaginary to envelop itself in an ambiguity of genre. *Tavolino* ("small table" in Italian) is a masculine noun, Cleopatra is female. And to stress the idea of playful sensuality already suggested by the curvy and sinuous forms of the object. The stand darts up to support the top in an apical position: like the common image of Cleopatra played by Elizabeth Taylor in Mankiewicz's film of 1963, where it is above all the head and the face to startle us into recognition.

Memphis Collection

Sherazade

Thermal carafe
Ettore Sottsass
1996
2001 product re-engineering
Alessi

In the great collection of Arab tales *A Thousand-and-One Nights* Sherazade is the young girl who, within the frame of the work, manages to avoid death by telling the King of Persia a different tale every night interrupting it at an opportune moment so as to leave the King with a longing to hear how it continued and how it ended. Symbol of both an almost infinite ability to fabricate stories and also an ability to dose them wisely, Sherazade lends her name, soaked with exotic resonance and fabled evanescence, to a carafe designed by Sottsass for Alessi intended to aid heat retention and, through a detailed study of the handle, calibrate the quantity of liquid poured. An ordinary household object is therefore charged to the hilt with arcane meaning and links in the imaginary the simple gesture of pouring a drink to the convivial and universal need to tell or listen to stories.

Alessi Collection

Show-business Icons

Like a game of loans, exchanges and anamorphic mirror refraction, some Italian design objects borrow their names from show-business icons: sometimes they are cult film characters acted by stars whose fame is linked to one specific role (Rita Hayworth's *Gilda*, Audrey Hepburn's *Sabrina*, Marlene Dietrich's *Lola*), at other times they are creatures which materialize as objects deriving from the papery thinness of comics (Guido Crepax's *Valentina*, Jean-Claude Forest's *Barbarella*), others still are media stars who, with their star aura, give new meaning to ordinary household articles (the *Black Josephine* cookie jar obviously hints at the cult singer Josephine Baker, the black Venus of Paris of the Twenties and Thirties, while the magazine rack named *Claudia Evangelista* is a kind of fusion of the names of two very well-known models like Claudia Schiffer and Linda Evangelista).

When objects take on names like these it is as though they were putting on a mask. As though they were submitting to a semiotic make-up in order to take part in the carnival of the imaginary. Sometimes the mask is only a homage from the designer to a heroine or a particularly loved figure, at other times instead the chosen name implies more subtle analogies.

But it is here, in the possible relationship that may be found between Marlene Dietrich's legs and the legs of the *Lola* lamp, or between Rita Hayworth's curves and the lines of the lamp and armchair which flaunt the name *Gilda*, that the naming game releases its full power in order to enrich meaning.

Gilda

Armchair
Carlo Mollino
1954
Zanotta

Zanotta Collection

From the moment Rita Hayworth slipped off her gloves to the rhythm of *Put the Blame on Mame* in the film directed by Charles Vidor in 1946 she became forever *Gilda*. Her image, when she dances or when she sings *Amado mio* with irresistible sensuality becomes the very icon of desire, eroticism and pleasure. Carlo Mollino's armchair pays homage to her myth evoking the baroque and carnal charm of that character and cult film.

Mollino's specialty was a procedure which he designed and patented himself for the cold wood curvature whose potential he was able to exploit in masterly fashion.
Its organic forms swell, flicker like flames, proliferate luxuriantly. Mollino never shirked any form of experimentation, producing for example three-legged chairs with bizarre curves, but also uninhibited imitations of the female anatomy: the backs of his chairs evoke womanly torsos or lewd hanging tongues, his bipartite chairs are splendid buttocks. The models for his table legs, some actually wearing high heels, were the Crazy Horse dancers.
If there is an "erotic" design, Mollino is surely its most inspired exponent.
(Claudia Neumann, *Design in Italia*, Rizzoli, Milan, p. 262)

Barbarella

Bureau
Ettore Sottsass
1965
Poltronova

Ettore Sottsass is the first Italian designer to perceive the signals of the emerging pop culture and to use a cross-media lexicon within his design practice.
This piece of furniture with bureau is inspired by the sexy intergalactic heroine of the fortieth century created for comics in 1962 by Jean Claude Forest (thinking of Brigitte Bardot as his model) and then transferred to the cinema screen in 1968 by Roger Vadim, with Jane Fonda dressed by Paco Rabanne who launches, with the costumes designed for this film, space fashion.
Sottsass perceives the euphoria for the future communicated by the comic strip and, before the film is made, transfers it to an object which, with its shape and materials (aniline varnished wood, anodized aluminum) could be part of a science fiction set.

Milan Triennale Collection

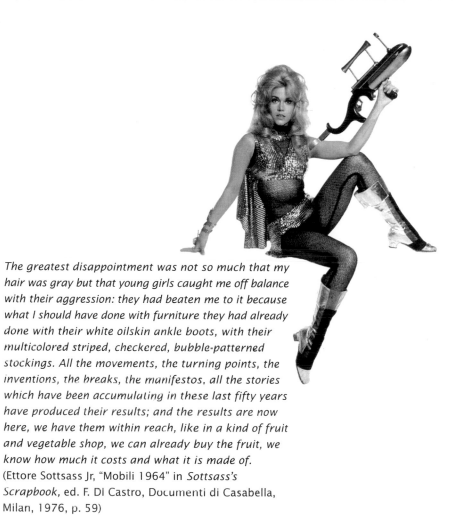

The greatest disappointment was not so much that my hair was gray but that young girls caught me off balance with their aggression: they had beaten me to it because what I should have done with furniture they had already done with their white oilskin ankle boots, with their multicolored striped, checkered, bubble-patterned stockings. All the movements, the turning points, the inventions, the breaks, the manifestos, all the stories which have been accumulating in these last fifty years have produced their results; and the results are now here, we have them within reach, like in a kind of fruit and vegetable shop, we can already buy the fruit, we know how much it costs and what it is made of. (Ettore Sottsass Jr, "Mobili 1964" in *Sottsass's Scrapbook*, ed. F. DI Castro, Documenti di Casabella, Milan, 1976, p. 59)

Valentine

Typewriter
Ettore Sottsass
Perry A. King
1969
Olivetti

Here too, as with *Barbarella*, Sottsass allows himself to be profitably influenced by the revolutionary cultural climate of the Sixties.

Here the allusion to the audacious comic-strip heroine created by Guido Crepax in 1965 is associated with the prototype of a new typewriter through the analogy of the innovative cultural values which are communicated: Crepax's *Valentina* is characterized by its aura of emancipation unlike traditional feminine models, but also by its ability to transform desire into action and imagination. Similarly Sottsass's *Valentina* is daring compared to the classical traditional line previously created by Olivetti and, at the same time, provides the increasing demand for writing which pervaded mass cultural scenarios in those years with a new portable artifact.

Alessandro Pedretti Collection

With its mixture of romanticism and irony, Gastone Rinaldi's chair alludes to Audrey Hepburn's character in Billy Wilder's film *Sabrina* (1954), where the actress plays a girl from a modest background who transforms herself into a sophisticated woman and makes a millionaire fall in love with her.

For me names have always been of fundamental importance. I have always consulted the dictionary of names to find out their origin and meaning. I have often used female names.
Gabri *is Gabriella, my eldest daughter.*
Stefi *is Stefania, my daughter who lives in New York.*
Lety *is my wife Letizia.*
Dafne, *instead, derives from the mythological world: in mythology she is a nymph loved by Apollo and transformed into a laurel bush, a little like this chair should have been with its light, graceful, folding, convertible shape.*
Aurora *is an outdoor chair for with soft shapes for sitting comfortably and enjoying the early morning.*
Elga *is a kooky girl I met with alternative ideas, she inspired me to make a chair made entirely from discs. And then* Nelly, Paola, Desy, Sara, Pilar....
Finally Sabrina *which is as spirited as Audrey Hepburn.*
(Gastone Rinaldi, December 2001)

Sabrina

Chair
Gastone Rinaldi
1970
Rima

Lola

Lamp
Paolo Rizzatto, Alberto Meda
1987
Luceplan

Lola is the name of the seductive cabaret singer Lola
Frolich, played by Marlene Dietrich, who drives an old
professor mad with love in Josef von Sternberg's film
The Blue Angel of 1930.

*Lola is Marlene Dietrich, they are her legs. There is
certainly a sexual reference, the triangle...it is as
strong as the character, it has three legs, it is very
flexible, supple, a little highly-strung, it is a short
name. A name dense with formal references.
I give a great deal of study to names when I design an
object. I think about it constantly, then when I begin to
know it in depth I name it, I find the name that allows
me to recognize it.
The name must recall and evoke the object.
The name is important, it is an integral part of the design.
Indeed the name is a design in itself.*
(Paolo Rizzatto, December 2001)

Milan Triennale Collection

Gilda

Lamp
In Suk II, Silvia Capponi
1993
Artemide

If Carlo Mollino's armchair *Gilda* derived above all an idea of irresistible sensuality from the immortal character played by Rita Hayworth, then this table lamp recalls the same myth but to emphasize instead the diffused lighting of the dark lady who moves in the shadows, while the colors and shape allude to the promise of pleasure that an icon such as *Gilda* spreads around her. The different aspect the lamp assumes according to whether it is switched on or off brings to mind one of the most famous lines of Charles Vidor, spoken by Glenn Ford's character: "A woman is like a cane with a retractable blade: she appears to be one thing and right before your eyes she turns into another."

Milan Triennale Collection

Claudia Evangelista

Magazine rack
Philippe Starck
1994
Kartell

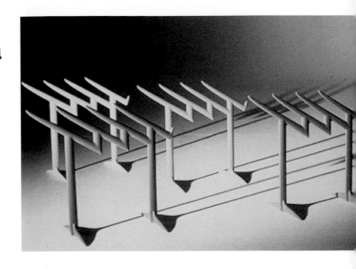

Milan Triennale Collection

Two legs, four arms. Turned upwards to "suspend,"
"to thread," "to prop" newspapers and magazines.
A comb-like structure, a shape that "stings."
The four arms, as the name implies, could be those of
Claudia (Schiffer) and (Linda) Evangelista.
A name + a surname.
Mixing, fusing, reuniting the two symbols of the
covers of glossies to name the stand intended to
contain the magazines which often show the two
models on their covers.
The container derives its name from its content.
With obvious irony.

Black Josephine

Cookie jar
Pierangelo Caramia
1995
Alessi

An object with a vibrant surface: curved, close,
spare, supple lines (the glass box) which spread
up to a perfectly smooth, continuous and rounded
(the steel lid) surface, imitating the shape
of a breast, with different colored knobs to
evoke nipples.

With its contrasts of colors and heat Pierangelo
Caramia's cookie jar condenses the two characteristics
most celebrated by the intellectuals who worshipped
Joséphine Baker: the suppleness of the body and the
crystal quality of the voice (cf. V. Mollica, *Chez
Joséphine. Omaggio a Joséphine Baker*, Editori del
Grifo, Montepulciano 1987, p. 7).

*New-generation designers create the object and give it
a name, they have an almost "animistic," "emotional"
approach which, according to D.Winnicott, belongs to
the area of transitional phenomena, understood as
that area of human, intermediate experience between
conceived and perceived things.*
(Alberto Alessi, December 2001)

Alessi Collection

The thing I desire most in life
is to own a large dictionary in
seven volumes, full of pictures.
But not to read: to lift it up
in my hands and weigh it
from time to time.
Words, we know, are heavy.
(Joséphine Baker)

Setting Up

Giancarlo Basili

Giancarlo Basili (1952) is one of the most important set designers in Italian cinema. He has worked with, among others, Gabriele Salvatores (*Nirvana*), Gianni Amelio (*Cosi ridevano*) and Nanni Moretti (*Palombella Rossa*, *La Stanza del figlio*).

The idea of the exhibition installation came from a reflection on cinema and above all Pedro Almodovar's film *All about my Mother*. I immediately pictured a room where memories pile up.

The space available was the Impluvium, a square and slightly static room, in the extraordinary Palazzo della Triennale.

I immediately felt the need to invade the space, to enlarge and magnify it.

I wanted to create the sensation of a large, almost gigantic space, where objects would emerge-re-emerge, like memories, and remain small, in such

103

a way that one could read them all on the same level, both the large and the very small ones.

For this reason, to create perspective, I made the walls taper towards the back of the room. This effect was then magnified and made tenfold by the use of the black-and-white checkered floor, slanted according to the rules of the central perspective. I covered the walls with Morris-style floral wallpaper, but enlarged to the point that the motif expressed a little of the spirit of the 60s and 70s. At the back of the room I placed a large screen, halfway between cinema (because the figures pro-

jected are on a large scale) and television (as though they were images moving through the room of a house).

When you come to think of it setting up an exhibition has many things in common with the making of scenery for films or theater. In both cases you have to be at the disposal of someone or something: a story in the case of a film, objects in the case of an exhibition. In fact, an exhibition too is a story, it has a plot, a script and a director. It uses objects like actors in a performance that produces emotions."

When Objects Have a Woman's Name

Essential Index

Adriana · small armchair · 1951 · Franco Albini · La Rinascente

Afrodisia · lamp · 1992 · Francesco Castiglione Morelli · Artemide

Aida · chair· 1987 · Andrea Branzi · Zanotta

Alda · armchair · 1966 · Cesare Casati · Enzo Hybsch · Comfort

Alesia · lamp · 1981 · Carlo Forcolini · Artemide

Alessia · chair · 1970 · Giotto Stoppino · Driade

Allegra · armchair· 1963 · Piero Ranzani · Elam

Anna · armchair· 1966 · Piero Ranzani · Elam

Anna G · corkscrew · 1994 · Alessandro Mendini · Alessi

Arianna · lamp · 1965 · Piero Brombin · Artemide

Arianne · lamp · 1994 · Luigi Trenti · Targetti

Auretta · hairdryer· 1956 · Alberto Rosselli · CGE

Aurora · chair · 1979 · Gastone Rinaldi · Thema

Aurora · lamp · 1983 · Perry King, Santiago Miranda · Arteluce

Bambole · armchair · 1972 · Mario Bellini · B & B

Barbarella ·bureau· 1965 · Ettore Sottsass · Poltronova

Babette · lamp· 1994 · Ufficio Tecnico · Candle

Berenice · lamp · 1985 · Paolo Rizzatto, Alberto Meda · Luceplan

Bianca · chair · 1996 · Franco Raggi · Schopenhauer

Bicia · armchair · 1969 · Carlo Bartoli · Arflex

Calliope · handle · 1980 · Alvaro Siza · Kleis

Carlotta · armchair · 1967 · Afra and Tobia Scarpa · Cassina

Carlotta · armchair · 1997 · Antonio Citterio · Flexform

Carmen · small armchair · 1986 · Enzo Mari · Zanotta

Carmencita · coffee pot · 1980 · Marco Zanuso · Lavazza

Carola · table· 1968 · Giovanni Offredi · Bazzani

Carolina · lamp · 1958 · Luigi Caccia Dominioni · Azucena

Cassiopea · small sofa · 1961 · Raffaella Crespi · Elam

Cassiopea · drinking glass · 1982 · Marco Zanuso Jr. · Memphis

Celestina · chair · 1978 · Marco Zanuso · Zanotta

Charlotte · small armchair· 1968 · Sergio Asti · Zanotta

Charlotte · piece of furniture· 1987 · Martine Bedine · Memphis

Charlotte · chaise longue · 1997 · Vico Magistretti · Campeggi

Chiara · lamp · 1967 · Mario Bellini · Flos

Cibele · lamp · 1998 · Andrea Anastasio · Artemide

Circe · lamp · 1985 · Carlo Forcolini · Artemide

Claudia Evangelista · magazine rack· 1994 · Philippe Starck · Kartell

Clea · small armchair· 1997 · Kristiina Lassus · Zanotta

Cleopatra · small table· 1987 · Marco Zanuso Jr. · Memphis

Corinna · bedside table· 1985 · Ignazio Gardella · Misura Emme

Cosima · lamp · 1998 · Christina Hamel · Segno

Costanza · lamp · 1986 · Paolo Rizzatto · Luceplan

Cristina · small armchair · 1962 · Raffaella Crespi · Elam

Cynthia · lamp · 1968 · Mario Marenco · Artemide

Dafne · chair · 1979 · Gastone Rinaldi · Thema

Daisy · lamp · 1985 · Martine Bedine · Memphis

Dalila · chair · 1980 · Gaetano Pesce · Cassina

Delfina · chair · 1974 · Enzo Mari · Driade

Denise · chair · 1987 · Nathalie Du Pasquier · Memphis

Diana · vase · Borek Sipek · Driade

Diva · mirror · 1984 · Ettore Sottsass · Memphis
Dolly · chair· 1996 · Antonio Citterio, Loew Oliver · Kartell
Ebe · lamp · 1962 · Sergio Asti · Artemide
Elda · armchair · 1965 · Joe Colombo · Comfort
Elena · chair· 1994 · Sottsass Associati · Zanotta
Elena · small table · Vico Magistretti · Artemide
Elettra · small armchair · 1954 · BPR · Arflex
Elisa · small armchair · 1964 · Giovanni Bassi, Giampiero Bassi · Poltronova
Erika · small armchair · 1992 · Giugiaro Design · Cinova
Ester · lamp · 1976 · Guido Rosati · Veart
Fedra · door handle · 1990 · Enrico Baleri with Margherita de Mitri· Kleis
Fiorenza · armchair · 1952 · Franco Albini · Arflex
Francesca · lamp · 1975 · Carlo Forcolini · Interni Luce
Franceschina · lamp · 1989 · Umberto Riva · Fontana Arte
Frine · lamp · 1970 · Studio Tetrarch · Artemide
Gaia · armchair · 1967 · Carlo Bartoli · Arflex
Galatea · lamp · 1998 · Andrea Anastasio · Artemide

Gemma · door handle · 1980 · Riccardo Dalisi · Kleis
Genni · chaise longue · 1935 · Gabriele Mucchi · Zanotta
Gilda · armchair · 1954 · Carlo Mollino · Zanotta
Gilda · lamp · 1993 · In Suk II, Silvia Capponi · Artemide
Gilda · lamp · 1998 · Enrico Franzolini · Palluccoitalia
Ginestra · chair · 1992 · P. Scarzella, P. Rasulo · Zanotta
Ginevra · chair · 1979 · Achille, Pier Giacomo Castiglioni · Bonacina
Giona · lamp · 1973 · Giorgina Castiglioni · Bilumen
Giorgia · armchair · 1994 · Ufficio Tecnico · Interflex
Giovi · lamp· 1982 · Achille Castiglioni · Flos
Giulietta · armchair · 1958 · BBPR · Arflex
Giunone · lamp · Vico Magistretti · Artemide
Graziella · bicycle · 1963 · Ufficio Tecnico · Carnielli
Greta · armchair · 1989 · Gilberto Corretti · Bianchi&Bruni
Iride · modular system · 1967 · Luca Meda · Molteni
Irma · chair · 1979 · Achille Castiglioni · Zanotta
Isetta · car · 1953 · Ermenegildo Preti · Iso Spa

Jessica · chair · 1994 · D'Urbino Lomazzi-Studio DDL · Zerodisegno
Juliette · chair · 1987 · Hannes Wettstein, Baleri&Associati · Baleri Italia
Juliette · chair · 1987 · Massimo Iosa Ghini · Memphis
La Marie · chair · 1998 · Philippe Starck · Kartell
Lady · armchair · 1951 · Marco Zanuso · Arflex
Lara · lamp · 1998 · Vico Magistretti · Artemide
Leopolda · small armchair · 1997 · Kostantin Grcic · Montina
Linda · chair · 1970 · Gastone Rinaldi · Rima
Linda · chair · 1974 · DDL · Zanotta
Linda · sanitary fittings · 1977 · Achille Castiglioni · Ideal Standard
Lisa · armchair· 2000 · Perry King, Santiago Miranda · Baleri Italia
Lola · lamp · 1987 · Paolo Rizzatto, Alberto Meda · Luceplan
Lola · chair · 1997 · Pierluigi Cerri · Poltrona Frau
Lori · chair · 1995 · Andrea Branzi · Zanotta
Lovely Rita ·shelf/bookcase· 1996 · Ron Arad · Kartell
Lucilla · lamp · 1994 · Paolo Rizzatto · Luceplan

Lucrezia · chair · 1984 ·
Marco Zanini · Memphis
Luigiona · vase· 1960 ·
Sergio Asti · Seguso
Luisa · chair · 1950 · Franco
Albini · Poggi
Luisa · chair · 1970 · Marcello
Cuneo · Mobel Italia
Maddalena · armchair · 1962 ·
GPA Monti · Monti
Maddalena · armchair · 1962 ·
GPA Monti · Delta
Madonna · table · 1984 ·
Arquitectonica · Memphis
Maia · series of accessories·
1969 · Giotto Stoppino ·
Bernini
Mami · pots· 1999 · Stefano
Giovannoni · Alessi
Margherita · armchair · 1950 ·
Franco Albini · Vittorio
Bonacina
Margherita · chair · 1968 ·
Eugenio Gerli · Tecno
Margot · console table · 1986 ·
Claudio Caramel · Art'è
Maria Blanca · armchair ·
1997 · Fabrizio Ballardini,
Lucio Costanzi · Arflex
Marianna · small armchair ·
1976 · DDL · Zanotta
Marina · lamp · 1981 · Gregotti
Associati · Fontana Arte
Marina · chair · 1991 · Enzo
Mari · Zanotta
Medea · chair · 1955 · Vittorio
Nobili · Fratelli Tagliabue

Medusa · lamp · 1992 ·
Sergio Asti · Salviati
Medusa · lamp· 1997 ·
Giugiaro Design · Bilumen
Michela · lamp · 1958 · Annig
Sarian · Adrasteia
Mimì · chair · 1991 · Enrico
Baleri · Baleri Italia
Mirandolina · chair · 1992 ·
Pietro Arosio · Zanotta
Mirella · sewing machine ·
1957 · M. Nizzoli · Necchi
Miss B · chair · 1998 · Tito
Agnoli · Pierantonio Bonacina
Miss C.O.C.O · chair · 1999 ·
Philippe Starck · Cassina
Miss Global · chair · 1992 ·
Philippe Starck · Kartell
Miss Hot · bathrobe heater ·
1998 · Paolo Pedrizzetti ·
Tubes Radiatori
Miss Sissi · lamp · 1990 ·
Philippe Starck · Flos
Miss Trap · table · 1990 ·
Philippe Starck · Kartell
Miss Trip · chair · 1995 ·
Philippe Starck · Kartell
Molly · sofa· 1991 · Enrico
Baleri · Baleri Italia
Molly · small armchair · 2001 ·
Bertro-Panto · Zanotta
Moni · lamp · Achille
Castiglioni · Flos
Morgana · lamp · Marco
Zanuso Jr. · Oceano Oltreluce
Musa · lamp· 1995 · Rodolfo
Dordoni · Artemide

Nadia · chair · 1987 · Beppe
Caturegli · Memphis
Nara · table · 1993 · Vico
Magistretti · De Padova
Nastassja · chair · 1987 ·
Giovanni Levanti · Memphis
Nathalie · bed · 1978 · Vico
Magistretti · Flou spa
Nathalie · chair · 1987 ·
Nathalie Du Pasquier · Memphis
Nelly · lamp · 1985 · Roberto
Pamio · Leucos
Nena · chair · 1984 · Richard
Sapper · B & B Italia
Neptunia · small armchair ·
1953 · BBPR · Arflex
Nina · lamp · 1981 · Gae
Aulenti · Piero Castiglioni ·
Fontana Arte
Niobe · lamp · 1963 · Sergio
Asti, Sergio Favre · Artemide
Norma · armchair · 1988 ·
Massimo Iosa Ghini · Moroso
Olya · lamp · 1985 · Vico
Magistretti · O-luce
Olimpia · bookcase · 1970 ·
Cesare Casati, Emanuele
Ponzio · Sormani
Olimpia · lamp· 1982 · Marco
Albini, Franca Helg, Antonio
Piva · Sirrah
Olimpia · lamp · 1986 · Carlo
Forcolini · Artemide
Olivia · lamp · 1994 · Roberto
Lucci, Paolo Orlandini · Segno
Olympia · lamp · 1985 ·
Martine Bedin · Memphis

Olympia · lamp · 1988 · Denis Santachiara · Modular Domodinamica
Olympia · mirror · 1989 · Matteo Thun · Kartell
Orsola · lamp · 1977 · Vico Magistretti · Vistosi
Ottavia · lamp · 1994 · Luciano Balestrini, Paola Longhi · Luceplan
Pandora · accessories · 1986 · Antonia Astori · Driade Aleph
Paolina · lamp · 1958 · Ignazio Gardella · Azucena
Paolina · chair · 1986 · Enzo Mari · Pozzi Verga
Per Elisa · desk · 1988 · Roberto Collovà · Acierno
Polinnia · lamp · 1964 · BPR · Artemide
Regina · chair · 1991 · Paolo Deganello · Zanotta
Regina d'Africa · armchair · 1979 · Vico Magistretti · Alias
Rossella · lamp · 1985 · Marco Zanini · Memphis
Sabrina · chair · 1970 · Gastone Rinaldi · Rima
Sabrina · armchair · 1982 · Alessandro Mendini · Driade
Sally · small table · 1987 · Shiro Kuramata · Memphis
Sandy · piece of furniture · 1987 · Aldo Cibic · Memphis
Sara · lamp · 1993 · Pierluigi Cerri · Candle

Scilla · chair· 1958 · Pierluigi Spadolini · ICS
Selene · chair · 1968 · Vico Magistretti · Artemide
Sherazade ·thermos 1996 · Ettore Sottsass · Alessi
Sibilla · handle· 1992 · Vico Magistretti · Olivari
Sibilla · small armchair· 1992 · Giovanni Lauda · Play Line
Signorina Chan · chaise longue · 1986 · Carlo Forcolini · Alias
Sophia · desk · 1985 · Aldo Cibic · Memphis
Susanna · small armchair· 1983 · Gabriele Mucchi · Zanotta
Susy · small armchair· 1956 · T. Ammannati, G. Vitelli · Rossi di Albizzate
Talia · small armchair· 1963 · BBPR · Arflex
Teresa · chair · 1989 · Enzo Mari · Lema
Tina · lamp · 1994 · Perry King, Santiago Miranda · Sirrah
Titania · lamp · 1989 · Paolo Rizzatto, Alberto Meda · Luceplan
Tizianella · door handle · 1959 · Sergio Asti, Sergio Favre · Olivari
Tonietta · chair · 1981 · Enzo Mari · Zanotta
Valentina · lamp · 1985 · DDL · Valenti

Valentine · typewriter· 1969 · Ettore Sottsass · Olivetti
Vanessa · bed · 1962 · Afra and Tobia Scarpa · Gavina, Knoll International
Veronica · lamp · 1979 · Giancarlo Frattini · Luci
Veronica · lamp · 1980 · Damiano Alberti · Ycami
Victoria · armchair · 1966 · Leonardo Fiori · Zanotta
Victoria · sofa · 1982 · Mario Bellini · Cassina
Viola · lamp · 1977 · Luigi Caccia Dominioni · Azucena
Viola · chair · 1997 · Tamar Ben David · Zanotta
Zelda · sofa · 1960 · Sergio Asti · Poltronova

We thank the following companies

Alessi · Arflex · Artemide · B & B · Bilumen · Bottecchia Cicli srl · Cassina · CGE · Driade · Flos · Kartell · Kleis · Luceplan · Medea · Memphis · Necchi · Olivetti · Poggi · Poltronova · Fratelli Tagliabue · Zanotta

For their kind collaboration

Francesca Appiani (Museo Alessi) · Anna Bartoli · Carlo Bartoli · Elena Bellini · Gianluca Borgesi (Zanotta) · Carlo Forcolini · Galleria del Design e dell'Arredamento Cantù · Roberto Gennari · Barbara Lehmann (Archivio Storico Cassina) · Alessandro Pedretti · Gastone e Letizia Rinaldi · Rodrigo Rodriquez · Simona Romano (Museo Kartell) · Giovanna Solinas (Artemide) · Antonio Turati (Bottecchia Cicli srl) · G. Villa

and also

Claudio Canova · Arianna Lelli Mami · Enrico Mastrapasqua · Paolo Pelanda

Photographic Credits

Archivio fotografico della Triennale di Milano
Fotografie di: Amendolagine e Barracchia pp. 34, 36, 38 (bottom), 40 (right), 42 (bottom), 44, 50, 51, 65, 67, 69, 72, 77, 79, 86, 90, 92, 96

Aldo Ballo pp. 64 (bottom), 66, 76 (right)
Ballo&Ballo p. 63
Archivio Bellini pp. 58, 59
Mario Carrieri p. 80
Farabola p. 37
Arianna Lelli Mami, graphic montage p. 38 (top)
Pernette Perriand 1961, G61082N, ADAGP 2000, p. 61
Photomovie pp. 42 (top), 78 (top), 83 (right), 89, 91, 94 (top), 95 (bottom), 99
Alberto Martini, drawing, p. 81
Mauro Masera pp. 46, 56, 57, 60, 62
Carlo Mollino, 1950-60, p. 49
M. Tursi, 1969, 75

Artemide, Catalogo '70, p. 78 (bottom)
Chez Joséphine. Omaggio a Joséphine Baker, by V. Mollica, Editori del Grifo, Montepulciano 1987, drawing by Paul Colin, p. 101
Compasso d'Oro, Design Italiano, Galleria del Design e dell'Arredamento Cantù, pp. 40, 53, 81 (top), 95 (top)
Mobili come architetture by Stefano Casciani, Arcadia Edizioni, 1984, pp. 47, 64
Stile Industria, Apr. 1958, n. 16, p. 76 (left)
Stile Industria, Dec. 1961, n. 35, p. 52
Jours de France, n. 626, 12 Nov. 1966, p. 55

Printed in March 2002
by La Grafica-Cantù- e-mail: lagrafica@cracantu.it
for Edizioni Charta